ENTREPRENEUR MINDSETS AND HABITS

TO GAIN FINANCIAL FREEDOM AND LIVE YOUR DREAMS

JAMES MOORE

CONTENTS

Introduction	v
1. Mindsets that Will Impede Progress	1
2. The Top Mindsets for Success	4
3. Find A Great Mentor	17
4. Changing the Game with Nutrition	20
5. Some Amazing Entrepreneurial Heroes of Our Time	29
6. You Reap What You Sow	50
7. 30-Day Plan	59
In Conclusion	63

© **Copyright 2018 - James Moore - All rights reserved.**

In no way is it legal to reproduce, duplicate, or transmit any part of this document in either electronic means or in printed format. Recording of this publication is strictly prohibited and any storage of this document is not allowed unless with written permission from the publisher. All rights reserved.

The information provided herein is stated to be truthful and consistent, in that any liability, in terms of inattention or otherwise, by any usage or abuse of any policies, processes, or directions contained within is the solitary and utter responsibility of the recipient reader. Under no circumstances will any legal responsibility or blame be held against the publisher for any reparation, damages, or monetary loss due to the information herein, either directly or indirectly.

Respective authors own all copyrights not held by the publisher.

Legal Notice:

This book is copyright protected. This is only for personal use. You cannot amend, distribute, sell, use, quote or paraphrase any part or the content within this book without the consent of the author or copyright owner. Legal action will be pursued if this is breached.

Disclaimer Notice:

The information in this book is the opinion of the author and is based upon the author's personal experiences and observations. The author does not assume any liability whatsoever for the use of, or the inability to use any or all information contained in this book, and accepts no responsibility for any loss or damages of any kind that may be incurred by the reader as a result of actions arising from the use of information found within this book. Use the information at your own risk. No promises of cures, capabilities, weight loss results, or otherwise are given by the author, herein.

INTRODUCTION

"A success is anyone who is realizing a worthy predetermined ideal, because that's what he or she decided to do ... deliberately. But only one out of 20 does that! The rest are 'failures." – Earl Nightingale

Welcome to my title. I am so thrilled you could join me here. I'm so excited to share these ground-breaking ideas with you, and so that you can be the best you can be in the entrepreneurial field of your choice.

So, why is it that some individuals can shine in any sphere they choose to give themselves to, and others just cannot manage even a glimmer of success, despite their definite talents? It seems unfair, really.

But, in truth, research shows us that it's actually the way that individuals think about their potential and skills that really counts most. In fact, historically speaking, many of those who have achieved real greatness have worked extremely hard to get to their end goals. And, it's also true that many were told that they would never amount to anything at all, by friends, colleagues, family and/or peers. The difference was that they believed that they could achieve their goals and worked extremely diligently to do so. Walt Disney who created Disneyland in the USA is a prime example of an individual who never gave up on his dreams. His belief in himself (and others) was profound and inspirational, to say the least.

Of course, we'd all like to know the "magical" secret to success, but the real reality is that there are actually so many different factors that must be taken into account, to what makes one a truly successful human being. It's definitely true that hard work and dedication are so important in reaching success. But there's more to success than just plugging away, day after day. Maintaining a focus-driven mindset is pivotal, and can be the difference between success and failure, especially in the long-term.

Unfortunately, some individuals believe that, basically, when it comes to talents and abilities, you are what you are, and that those things are final, in the whole scheme of things. So, they say that: you are already as smart you are, as hardworking as you are, and there's nothing you can possibly do to change these detrimental characteristics of your 'lot' in life. That's what we call a *solid mindset*.

Others have a different story to tell. These people with the opposing view have a "sprouting" or *growth mindset*, and they believe, wholeheartedly, that with motivation and sheer perseverance, you can grow your intellect, expand your skill set, improve your persona, and beat anything that might stand in the way of goals and dreams. In fact, growth mindset people can already see what is needed for getting ahead, and they gain this potential via the input of real, old-fashioned, hard effort and work.

This fact was proven by the well-known research achieved

by renowned Stanford psychologist, Carol Dweck. In a fascinating study, the message given was clear.

She noted that, "*It's all about your mindset. Successful people tend to focus on growth, solving problems, and self-improvement, while unsuccessful people think of their abilities as fixed assets and avoid challenges.*"

Other studies also back up Dweck's findings. But it was profoundly surmised that the long and short-term achievements were definitively changed through this type of mindset. In fact, her work suggested that those with a growth mindset would be substantially more successful in the future, with notably bigger effects in the short term, as well. Dweck also noted that individuals who took on a growth mindset had both diminished stress and anxiety levels, and also an enhanced self-esteem, overall. Generally, these individuals were also in better overall physical health. This is a massive game changer in itself, for both health and success, which is all totally controlled by the mind.

It was also learned, that just telling high school students in a single class about having a growth mindset (and its effects), gave large positive effects. And, these were seen on both a physical level, and on a psychological one, just a year later. In fact, there were effects to those individuals, long-term. Learning that there was a "different story" to tell internally, was actually shown to be a pivotal factor in the study. It's a wonderful and positive actualization that young students can take away. It can change the way they live, think, feel, and also create wealth.

1
MINDSETS THAT WILL IMPEDE PROGRESS

Okay, so if you truly want to get rich or be successful in whatever field you wish, you must look toward the future, and make sure that you're not constantly going over where you are in the present point in time. So, this means you'll need to make goals, and some might span years into the future, not just mere weeks or months. According to research, the lengthier you stretch your thinking, sending it into the future, the richer you will eventually become.

In fact, future set goals implement bigger questions like, *"How can I make half a million dollars?"* as opposed to short-term problems, like, *"How am I going to pay my rent this month?"*

Don't Be Afraid of Change

Rather than being scared of what might be, it's very important to view change as an opportunity for potentially-positive outcomes, instead.

Researcher Smith surmises, *"The problem with the middle class is it assumes change will be negative most of the time."* He goes on to say, *"Millionaires assume that all change, positive or negative, will benefit them."* Looking at growth in the changes that happen allows for positivity to ensue, Smith states, *"Confidence is acquired through preparation and hard work,"* and he goes on to say, *"Confidence is the result of working on yourself. It is the benefit of proving yourself to yourself. It is knowing you can handle whatever comes your way."*

Don't Have the Need for Instant Gratification

To build wealth is time-consuming; it takes effort, and patience, too. In fact, during his research, Smith realized that millionaires were great at putting their temporary comfort on the backburner. This went hand-in-hand to seeking out a long-term, real, financial freedom.

He states, *"Middle-class people want instant gratification. I was like that for many years. Whatever I wanted, I charged to my credit card or put a little bit down and made payments on the balance. Now I wait for the things I want because my goal is more freedom, not comfort."* He added, *"Rich and very rich people have developed the discipline of delayed gratification."*

Don't Try & Do Everything Yourself

Setting up multiple streams of income is a key factor. Doing everything yourself is not attainable, especially when you need other vantage points, in terms of skill or knowledge basis.

Smith states, *"The belief that you must do everything yourself puts extreme limits on your financial potential. Having a belief that no one can do it as well as you is ignorance. The world is full of talented people."*

It's really crucial not to flip out that a certain task or skill won't be done correctly if you don't do it yourself. In fact, it's really pivotal when you can place innate faith into people who work for you. Delegation gives you a chance to improve your end result, or final outcome.

2

THE TOP MINDSETS FOR SUCCESS

THE BELIEF IN GIVING

Smith states, "Most millionaires believe in the law of sowing and reaping. They see money as a seed. Millionaires know that if they are generous, they will receive more in return."

Many brilliant millionaires and even billionaires have turned into philanthropists. These include the likes of Mark Zuckerberg, Richard Branson, Bill Gates, Warren Buffet, and Elon Musk, who have done this.

The Billionaire Mindset

The biggest aspect that gets negated time and time again is: You must ALWAYS know your purpose (or focus).

It's written in **bold** here for the purpose of remembrance. IT IS QUITE LITERALLY the most important thing you need to remember. The individuals who pursue a dream or have a main focus on their end goal/s in life are, actually, the wealthiest and happiest people in the world. Additionally, because they love their work, they are happy to focus upon it, for the long-term. Their passion is provoked, and so they put all of their effort in. Effort and perseverance; plus passion, is a great winning combination for wealth creation.

Usually, it's true that: if you're not making sufficient income at your job, it is because you are doing something you most probably don't like. So, it's also true to say that: when you can earn a substantial income doing something you enjoy, you have found your main focus, the one that's right for you.

Find Your Purpose by Following These 5 Easy Steps:

1. Make a list of everything that makes you happy, or that creates a feeling of joy for you. Do 10.

2. Circle the items on your list that include a skill, and then write that skill next to the point of focus.

3. Rank each circled item in the order of happiness they bring to you. Give the top one 10 points, and each one after that a point lower than 10. So, 10, 9, 8, 7, etc., in descending order, as required.

4. Now, you need to do this again, but order them ranking the top 10 circled items, in terms of those with the highest income potential. Give the top one 10 points, and each one after that a point lower. So, 10, 9, 8, 7, etc., in descending order, as required.

5. Totalling the two ranked columns. The highest score represents a potential main focus for your life.

They Never Believe That Failure is Failure

Rich people don't believe that failure is failure. In fact, they see failure as a movable block to their success, and believe that it also provides multiple opportunities that can be learned from. A billionaire has ALWAYS failed numerous times in their journey to accumulate wealth. Henry Ford, the founder of the Ford Motor Company said, *"Failure is just a resting place. It is an opportunity to begin again more intelligently."*

They Know That Giving Up Is Not an Option

Millionaires and billionaires continue with the growth mindset that helps them get to where they want to be. They are completely goal centred and focused in achieving their vision. They (absolutely) will not give up until they achieve them. Perseverance and sustainable effort are always the key here.

They Think Big & Dream Big

Whether you love him or hate him, it doesn't matter. The point is, he is a very successful businessman, one who has achieved remarkable goals. In the words of Donald Trump, *"I like thinking big. If you're going to be thinking anything then you might as well think big."*

They Have Empowering Beliefs about Wealth Creation

The most important aspect is this: **Rich people are comfortable with money.** They are happy spending it and they love it. Having thoughts of never enough, or I won't be able to... etc., are completely negating. Having an empowering mindset about wealth creation will allow you to accept its flow of it into your life. There are many spiritual and mindset coaches who teach this: if you believe it's true, then it's already done. Even athletes take on mindsets that help, not negate their goals.

They Manifest Their Own Destiny

A true believer believes that they can create their wealth using a combination of thoughts which is then accentuated by a massive action, or follow-through. They are the master of their own creation, quite literally so.

They Take Complete Responsibility

Experiencing setbacks is part of the journey, and psychologically, they know that it's just a hiccup in a big plan. A well thought out plan that will ultimately come to fruition through hard work and perseverance. Losing sight of their end goal is never an option.

They Take Some Risks

Billionaires play the wealth game to win at it. They allow opportunities to be utilized, with a mindset of not losing what they have. Sometimes, taking a gamble might pay off, and sometimes not. But failure, remember, is just a stepping stone. They see it as a learning curve that can and will be pushed through.

They Have the Belief That Their Wealth is Abundant

They realize that wealth is available everywhere in the world, and that if you provide massive value to other people, then it will build, over time. They do not, for one moment, believe that money is hard to come by. That would go against their dreams and end goals, which is NEVER an option.

They Realize That Education & Intelligence Don't Necessarily Matter In the Scheme of the Bigger Picture

It's true; money doesn't care about qualifications, credentials, or even your IQ score. Money is abundant when individuals find multiple opportunities to create value for others. It is the market that actually chooses where the wealth goes, and utilizing opportunity will help an individual to build wealth.

They Know That Wealth Builds When You Help Others

If you can help to alleviate a specific problem that individuals have, and do this on a large enough platform, then you WILL create more abundance for yourself.

"You can get everything in life you want if you will just help enough other people get what they want." – Zig Ziglar

It's true. Mindset is EVERYTHING. You first need to believe something before you can achieve it. It's pivotal, actually. Because then your whole being will react and aid the cause, therefore, helping you to set the scene for your goals through purposeful, hard effort and actioning. After that, it snowballs... and then you repeat your efforts until it's done.

Reaching Out

It might seem true to many people that the purpose of product development is a first priority, but Greg Gianforte (master bootstrapper) claims this is the wrong approach. He moved to Montana with his wife and family after he sold a previous company. Gianforte became restless and decided it was time to start again.

His focus laid on the technology sector where his vast experience was most active. Rather than starting a prototype for a new product or service and then seeking out funding, he began speaking on the phone with his potential customers. This led to many conversations about what sort of products these customers were willing to buy.

After spending a month of making phone calls, Gianforte spent approximately two months coding the new product his newfound customers had said they "would" purchase. He claims his new company, *RightNow Technologies*, was in a stable financial situation from the very start.

In fact, Gianforte's new business produced cloud-based software for the larger consumer businesses, and was then sold to Oracle back in 2011.

Finding New Markets for Existing Products

Rock 'n Roll wasn't invented by Sam Phillips, the founder of *Sun Records*. However, his small, Memphis-based record label is evermore linked to its foundations.

Phillips founded his recording studios, and in due course, his record label was known as a way of being able to capture the country's interaction of the blues music he'd become familiar with while performing as a DJ.

There was a vast pool of talent he had faith in, while still knowing most of the country was unfamiliar with, or never heard of the said acts. He fashioned a relaxed recording studio environment, which had distinctive acoustics to capture and preserve this new found talent.

Phillips went on to unearth stars like Johnny Cash, Jerry Lee Lewis, Carl Perkins, and Elvis, and he turned out to be a music icon and thus, became a prosperous entrepreneur from his endeavors.

Building Business through Networking

A good many entrepreneurs speak of the importance of networking. However, few are as specific of why networking is of such significance as Jason Nazar is (the co-founder and CEO of *Docstock.com*).

During an interview on "*MyTreat Blog,*" Nazar states he owes his success, and in particular, the formation and evolution of his current company, to the efforts he made in networking.

He says it was his networking efforts which helped raise $4 million in funding. He states it also helped to locate his co-founder from which he was able to build the bulk of his organization.

Nazar gives weighty advice to other entrepreneurs when it comes to making use of networking in business. First of all, it is crucial to measure the return on investment you will get from any networking efforts.

Secondly, something of value must be given first when making initial connections, rather than asking for something in the beginning.

Give Without Assuming a Return

Although it might appear a contradiction to the last point, it really works. According to James Altucher, an author, hedge fund manager and technology entrepreneur, he sticks to his belief that numerous opportunities come in your direction when something is offered without initially looking for payback.

Altucher states he frequently sends out ideas to people with whom he wishes to do business with, or people he admires and wishes to meet. On both occasions, he asks for nothing in return. Regularly, he doesn't receive any responses, although he says, on occasions the results are magical.

Altucher sent Jim Cramer (an investment expert and co-founder of *"TheStreet.com"*) a list of proposed article topics. From this, Altucher received the invitation to start being a contributing writer.

The ultimate result was that *"TheStreet.com"* later invested in one of Altucher's websites called "Stockpickr.com" which they later went on to buy from him.

Controlling Your Vision

Alibaba, the giant, Hong Kong-based, wholesale, e-commerce site founder Jack Ma (also known as Ma Yun), is the founder and leading hand behind its recognition and economic success. However, *Alibaba's* path toward acceptance outside mainland China wasn't easy.

There were many complaints of counterfeit and fake branded items being sold on the site. The problem was vastly aggravated as *Alibaba* attempted to position itself as a viable and reputable site, and one in which other businesses would use as a wholesale merchandising source.

When *Alibaba* considered going public with an IPO, another challenge loomed. Ma wanted to keep tight control of his company, and his team of executives which were already in place.

This can be difficult when new investors enter the overall picture. Many investors wish to have their input on how the company is run, especially once they have invested their hard-earned money.

Jack Ma had confidence in his vision for his company, and also the culture he created to get the job done.

Understanding Brand Power

In the late 70s and early 80s, and when the original "Star Wars" movies were released, many people only saw it as a pop-culture phenomenon. The successful film franchise which followed, though, actually created an entirely new market based on science fiction and fantasy.

George Lucas, the creator and filmmaker, had a vision of much more. To him, the first and second trilogy of films became a powerful brand. This brand became the springboard for many lucrative licensing deals. This included everything from toys and video games, to memorabilia and live attractions.

Lucas sold the Star Wars franchise and Lucas film in 2012 to Disney, for a record 4.05 billion.

After this, Lucas never lost faith or his interest in robust and profitable brands. He invested 10 million in the highly-successful café chain we now all know as "Starbucks."

Focus Energies on the Good of Your Business

Jay Z is known well, and not just for his music. He has best-selling albums, nightclubs, a clothing line, and a sports franchise, plus more. The rapper is also known for his astute business acumen.

His success is partly based on his focus on his refusal to spend time on anything which doesn't develop his entrepreneurial ventures. Zack O'Malley Greenburg, a Forbes staff writer, says it was this focus which caused Jay Z to decline the involvement in a book Greenburg was writing about him.

On the flip-side, Jay Z chose to publish his own book and was able to profit directly from telling his own story.

A vast number of people might contemplate this outlook as being short-sighted, although the question remains... on how many occasions have we allowed others to divert our focus and energies away from our businesses, and in the long-run, what does it cost us?

Always Maintaining Quality Control

Lionel Puoilâne was obsessed from the age of fourteen, once he began an apprenticeship in the family bakery until his death in 2002. His obsession was with the quality of bread that bore his family's name.

Puoilâne soon became a world-famous artisan for crafted bread that was baked in traditional wood-fired ovens.

When international demand for his bread grew, he still refused to turn to the mass production of his products. To maintain his quality, he insisted each loaf was still to be handcrafted by bakers who were personally trained in his techniques.

Even while experimenting with more up-to-date techniques, and with the expansion of his bakery operations, Puoilâne's focus on maintaining his quality control in his business never faltered. His traditions and standards continue at the hands of his daughter, Apollonia.

Setting Your Products Apart

Creating a product which stands apart is nothing new. Back in 1783, George and William Penrose undertook to produce crystal glass as fine as any, within mainland Europe. Soon the *Waterford* brand was born.

The brothers came up with a secret technique which combined glass and minerals which produced a crystal that actually "sang." It made their crystal renowned when it was tapped with the finger, and this distinct tone could be heard.

Waterford crystal is likewise known for its deep and elaborate carvings. These are created by skilled artisans which gives it its distinctive appearance.

The *Waterford* brand was so beloved and valued, that even when the factory closed in the 1850s due to hard times, the unsurpassed superiority of Waterford Crystal has never been forgotten.

Almost a hundred years later, and *Waterford Crystal* was revived back to its former glory with the returning of the crystal to the town in Ireland. Taking its name from the town it was made in.

Taking Ownership

Oprah Winfrey experienced lots of success as a well-known broadcaster, and in the entertainment industry too, even before launching *The Oprah Winfrey Show*, back in 1986.

After several radio and TV jobs, she hosted a successful chat show in Baltimore, and later there was another show in Chicago which went on to beat Phil Donahue in the local TV ratings.

Oprah even starred in the movie, "The Color Purple" alongside Whoopi Goldberg which was directed by Steven Spielberg. However, it wasn't until she took possession of her syndicated talk show from ABC that Oprah's entrepreneurial skills started to show. Her own production company eventually went on to produce other TV and film projects.

Winfrey's entrepreneurial mentality ultimately led her to launch a magazine and her own TV network.

The Importance of Finding the Correct Mentor

One thing I've come to learn while becoming an entrepreneur, is that good things are very rarely accomplished all by yourself. In fact, success (more often than not) hinges on receiving the best advice and support from the people who really do know.

At some stage, we all have mentors in our lives, even if we realize it or not. The earliest mentors are naturally parents, grandparents or other family members. These are followed by teachers and some employers, too. All great doctors, lawyers, teachers, and business leaders almost certainly learned their craft from another who preceded them.

When you have access to a mentor, you will benefit from learning from another person who's reached the stage that you are attempting to get to.

They understand all the sacrifices which have to be made, along with pitfalls which must be avoided. They are also well-versed in challenges which arise along the way.

Occasionally, we think of mentors as people with the "correct" contacts. However, I find it's more significant to find "that" someone who can teach you the skills and offer advice in your particular field.

Mentors can have a remarkable impact on your self-confidence, too. Anytime you venture out and try something new, you will have a lot of self-doubt and questioning involved in the whole process. Occasionally, it is possible to overcome uncertainty on your own. Nevertheless, it's a lot easier if you receive a few supportive words from someone you hold with great respect.

3

FIND A GREAT MENTOR

Find a Person Who Listens

MANY PEOPLE WILL PROBABLY BE READY TO OFFER ADVICE without taking the time to first understand you and your situation. A good example is: I've been told my business must lower prices, raise prices, expand into new areas, or should be closed altogether.

The problem is, none of these people who offered their advice bothered to ask any questions first. So, I suggest, when searching for a mentor, only focus on those who are likely to ask helpful questions and will pay attention to your answers. This is necessary, before they dish out advice to you.

Look for Individuals Who've Walked the Walk

Experience is priceless. There are plenty of people who can talk a good game, although you need to discover a person who has actual, "real-world" experience in your field.

Good mentors will share their experiences and can help apply what they've learned to your own path using their knowledge.

Watch Out for Hidden Agendas

On certain occasions, some advisors might not have your best interests at heart. An example being: I was once told to avoid becoming involved in a particular business. I found that the individual (all along) had planned on opening the same business themselves!

Trusting your gut can be advisable when it comes to receiving advice, especially when they are excessively persistent with their advice. You need to be aware of individuals who aren't really trying to help you. A real mentor will not force anything onto you, or try to sway you to the point of feeling your gut wrench (beginning to tell you something is up.)

Be Bold & Respectful

In some specific cases, any mentor-mentee relationship will form naturally. When this happens, it's beautiful, but on occasions, you might need to take the matter into your own hands. You are in control of your "enterprise."

Consider people who you admire, ones who share the same qualities and values. Then, reach out to them, and politely invite them to coffee or lunch (at their convenience).

I find people are usually flattered by the fact someone has spent the time to look them up to ask for advice. Their time is of importance, so always be respectful of their decisions. No one owes you anything. It's nice if someone takes time to talk with you. Time is money, so they are being extremely kind if they are taking time away to guide you. In fact, you might be able to help them, too. Just don't "give away" everything.

Mentors Who Will Tell You When You Are Wrong

Mentors who agree with all you say probably won't help you make any forward progress. If you are serious about growing, search for a mentor who will support and challenge you in equal measure.

Some of the most important conversations are those where you are pushed outside of your comfort zone.

The final thing about mentors is, don't forget to put yourself in their position. Situations might arise when someone reaches out to you. None of us reach our destinations alone. If you've been privileged enough to find success, you should find the time to share your acumen and experiences with others. Of course, you don't have to tell them everything, but a few tips or tricks might help.

4

CHANGING THE GAME WITH NUTRITION

Our body changes completely every 7 years! How amazing. This means each and every cell will be renewed and exchanged for another one during this period. I wasn't aware of this and am still amazed by it.

In any entrepreneurial (or success) books, this topic is very rarely (if ever) mentioned. However, I feel it can be one of the most critical areas to talk about. When you have a healthy mind and body, your productivity can increase... miles ahead of your competition.

An essential part of a healthy lifestyle is healthy eating. Most people though, are liable to only think of health and nutrition in connection with weight loss and health, in general. It is very few who connect their eating habits with work productivity.

Scientists at Brigham Young University conducted research which revealed employees with an unhealthy diet were 66% more likely to lose productivity than the healthy eating co-workers they studied.

Foods we eat have a direct impact on our overall work performance. So, if you wish to increase your productivity, it is time to pay close attention to your overall eating habits.

Poor Nutrition Affects Performance

Abundant scientific research confirms that the foods we eat will affect our health and longevity. A modern diet is full of processed foods and usually lacks the most essential nutrients. Such diets lead to the development of heart disease, diabetes, hypertension, and obesity.

These chronic health conditions result in productivity losses at home and at work while also having negative impacts on your quality of life. When your body performs poorly, your mind will suffer too. This is because it can't function properly.

An unhealthy diet will not provide enough energy for your everyday requirements, quite the reverse, actually. Leading to:

- overall fatigue
- poor mental health
- irritability
- the likelihood of stress and depression increasing
- energy levels decreasing

- clear thought becoming harder
- efficiency being difficult to maintain

A Healthy Diet & Productivity

Healthy eating necessitates eating a variety of foods. These (preferably raw) should be from all food groups, which gives a balance of nutrients to maintain health and energy. These foods will include proteins, carbohydrates, fats, water, vitamins, and minerals.

Healthy eating will have a positive impact on new cell development in the brain, along with many other numerous health benefits.

Reducing Levels of Stress

Studies reveal people who continually maintain healthy eating habits are less prone to suffer from anxiety, depression or have mood swings. When eating healthy foods, you can cope with stress quicker and you are able to concentrate on your work to a higher degree. Focus is easier and energy levels are sustainable.

Staying Physically & Mentally Active

The vast nutrients which are presented in food not only affect our physical health, but also our mental health. An influx of healthy nutrients improves brain functions that allow us to handle many work challenges.

In a nutshell, developing healthy eating habits helps you to succeed in both your personal life along with your professional life.

How can we avoid any adverse outcomes which are caused by poor nutrition, and then improve productivity?

We need to make smarter decisions about our diet. Foods which are harmful to health must be negated. We need to be choosing foods which are healthy, and make sure we include those which have an overall positive impact on our well-being.

Foods Which Decrease Productivity

The human brain consumes roughly 20% of the body's energy. When planning a diet, we ought to rely on scientific conclusions which explain how different foods will affect the brain. Ingredients from foods we consume either help us to focus and concentrate, or, in contrast, they have a negative impact on our aptitude to perform.

When you want your brain to perform at its best, junk food should be avoided.

The Principal Adversaries of Productivity Are:

Sugary Foods - Soda or candy gives you a short-term burst of energy, although later, you'll suffer from a sugar crash and can feel weak, anxious, or even confused. Other sugary foods might include: donuts, cakes, cookies, shortbread, and other bakery items.

Calorie Dense Foods - Hamburgers or fries are packed full of trans-fats and saturated fats. These make the digestive system work harder, while reducing levels of oxygen to the brain. These make us feel sleepy, sluggish, and they decrease overall work performance, too. If it's called junk food, then it is junk for your productivity.

Great Juicing Benefits

I'd love to list all foods which can aid in increasing productivity. However, that might take volumes to fully complete. If you're genuinely concerned about improving productivity, there's plenty of information which is searchable on the internet.

Highly recommended is an author named Stephen T. Chang. All of his books are, without question, surprising, and will benefit you immensely. Nevertheless, in this chapter, I'll talk about juicing as a quick and simple way to get your nutrients in, each day. Juicing is a quick and convenient start to boosting your productivity without taking up too much of your time.

Performance Level Boosting

When fruits and vegetables are broken down, this allows glucose to be formed which the body needs to function. The quicker foods can be broken down, the less energy is lost by the body.

When an individual drinks a juice, they get an immediate boost of energy which enhances the readily available nutrients. This boost of energy and nutrients will allow a person to function more proficiently on both a physical and cognitive level.

Fruits and vegetables which are in their freshest state can be used to create juices which provide maximum amounts of energy, and are fantastic nutrient additions with the least amount of waste.

Juices can be used as a healthy snack between meals, or they can even substitute for smaller meals if they are taken early enough in the day.

Through the use of a juicer or high-quality blender, you can drink at least three glasses of fresh juice each day. These can be prepared in advance and stored in the refrigerator to be consumed throughout the day.

The boost in overall health, as well as productivity, will become apparent, and you'll wish you knew this, years ago.

5 Easy Recipes for an Energy Boost to Get You Started:

Watermelon and Mint Juice: Ingredients

- 4 cups of cubed watermelon - seeds can be left in or removed
- 1/2 a cup of water
- 1/2 a cup of white sugar to taste - can use honey as a healthy alternative
- 1/2 a medium lime
- 24 fresh mint leaves
- a handful of ice cubes

Directions

- Add the watermelon, ice, and water to a blender and puree until smooth. Add sugar (or honey) to taste.
- Cut the lime slices and place half a lime slice into a glass along with some mint leaves.
- Pour and enjoy.

Breakfast Revitalizing Juice: Ingredients

- 2 medium lemons - peeled, seeded, and cut into quarters
- 2 medium carrots - washed and roughly chopped
- 2 medium apples - cored and quartered
- 2 medium beets - washed and trimmed, then chopped

Directions

- Pass all ingredients through a juicer and into a large glass.
- Pour into a glass and enjoy.

Cooler than Cucumber Juice: Ingredients

- 2 medium cucumbers - peeled, seeded, and then chopped
- 1/2 a medium lime - for juice
- 6 tablespoons of honey as a healthy alternative
- 2/3 of a cup of water
- a handful of ice cubes

Directions

- Add all the ingredients into a blender.
- Blend until smooth.
- Pour into a glass and enjoy.

Orange and Carrot Juice: Ingredients

- 2 pounds of carrots – organic, washed and trimmed
- 8 medium oranges - peeled

Directions

- Pass the carrots and oranges through a juicer and into a large glass.
- Add ice cubes.
- Pour into a glass and enjoy.

Healthy Orangeade Juice: Ingredients

- 6 tablespoons of honey (or to taste)
- 6 cups of water
- 1 1/2 cups of freshly squeezed orange juice
- 1/3 of a cup of freshly squeezed lemon juice
- ice cubes

Directions

- Mix well together until honey is mixed in well.
- Add a slice of watermelon for extra flavor.
- Pour into a glass and enjoy.

The food we eat influences many aspects of our life: our overall physical well-being, our mental health, and our work performance, too. Food can be used to your advantage.

If you practice proper nutrition which is based on nutritious foods, you can stay healthy and improve your overall productivity in the workplace and at home, as well. This is very important to do. Our partners, friends, families, and children also benefit from our practice. They can get the best of us too, because we feel good and have boosted energy. Your children will also learn the right way to go about nutrition as you influence their lives, positively, by being their role model.

5

SOME AMAZING ENTREPRENEURIAL HEROES OF OUR TIME

I THINK IT'S GREAT AFFIRMATION TO GO THROUGH SOME OF THE great icons of are time. Let the stories and quotes inspire you and notice how many of there quotes are quit similar and let that stick in your mind and overtime they will become your own mind sets.

Steve Jobs: February 24, 1955 to October 5, 2011

Steve Jobs is the founder of Apple Computer Corporation. His success story is really quite legendary. In fact, his mother placed him up for adoption immediately after he was born. And, she did this, just because he was "an unexpected baby."

He did go to college, but he eventually made the decision to drop out because of the costs involved.

"I didn't have a dorm room, so I slept on the floor in friends' rooms, I returned coke bottles for the 5¢ deposits to buy food with, and I would walk the seven miles across town every Sunday night to get one good meal a week at the Hare Krishna temple."

When he turned twenty, Steve Jobs and Steve Wozniak started a company in a garage on April 1, 1976. At the time, Steve saw a computer that Wozniak had made, just for his own use. So, Jobs then named their company "Apple" after a happy memory where he had spent his time as an orchard worker in Oregon, the prior summer.

In the same year, the men showed off the Apple-1 at *The Homebrew Computer Club* in California. A local store there offered to buy fifty machines. And, to financially back the production, the men had to sell their most loved possessions. Jobs sold his Volkswagen van and Wozniak sold his Hewlett-Packard scientific calculator.

The Apple II (second product) became such a popular hit that it is credited to be the best-selling computer in the 70s decade and for the early 80s. But, in 1982, his company sales lowered due to the fierce competition from IBM and their latest PC.

So, Apple Inc. began working on a new machine called the Macintosh. Brought to the public in 1984; by 1986, the Mac was a wonderful success. After a decade, and beginning with two experimental guys working in a garage, Apple Inc. had grown into a 2 billion dollar company, now employing four thousand employees.

Due to a power struggle within the company, Jobs was subsequently stripped of his duties in 1985, and it was in that same year that he left the company.

"It turned out that getting fired from Apple was the best thing that could have ever happened to me. The heaviness of being successful was replaced by the lightness of being a beginner again, less sure about everything. It freed me to enter one of the most creative periods of my life."

Steve Jobs is also the former Chairman and CEO of Pixar Animation Studios, which is distinctly famous for its production of animated films such as the very-popular *Toy Story*. The firm was eventually bought by Walt Disney Studios for 7.4 billion dollars in stock, and making Steve Jobs the biggest individual shareholder at the company, Disney.

Steve Jobs' Motivational Quotes:

"I'm convinced that about half of what separates successful entrepreneurs from the non-successful ones is pure perseverance."

"My favorite things in life don't cost any money. It's really clear that the most precious resource we all have is time."

"My model for business is The Beatles. They were four guys who kept each other's kind of negative tendencies in check. They balanced each other, and the total was greater than the sum of the parts. That's how I see business: great things in business are never done by one person, they're done by a team of people."

"Sometimes when you innovate, you make mistakes. It is best to admit them quickly, and get on with improving your other innovations."

"Your work is going to fill a large part of your life, and the only way to be truly satisfied is to do what you believe is great work. And the only way to do great work is to love what you do. If you haven't found it yet, keep looking. Don't settle. As with all matters of the heart, you'll know when you find it."

"Innovation distinguishes between a leader and a follower."

"Bottom line is, I didn't return to Apple to make a fortune. I've been very lucky in my life and already have one. When I was 25, my net worth was $100 million or so. I decided then that I wasn't going to let it ruin my life. There's no way you could ever spend it all, and I don't view wealth as something that validates my intelligence."

ENTREPRENEUR MINDSETS AND HABITS

Arnold Schwarzenegger: Born July 30, 1947

It's true, both his life and career have been a wonderful inspiration to so many around the entire globe, including brilliant roles in blockbusters like "The Terminator" and many more great roles. Additionally, boasting a solid political career, and being a hero with his bodybuilding inspiration, too. It seems, Schwarzenegger has been a true visionary and a motivator, a real hero of our time.

A True Visionary

"Let your imaginations take you where you really want to be."

Turn Thought to Action

"Once you have set a picture for you, no matter how weird it may seem initially, it sure has something for you in store, start working toward it. Take baby steps but be consistent in whatever you do."

Take Responsibility

"You need to question yourself as to what you want to do and how you are going to do it."

Never Give Up

"If you are obstinate enough to let your imaginations and vision flow,

there is absolutely no point of quitting, just because the path leading to success becomes uneven."

Some More of Arnold Schwarzenegger's Motivational Quotes:

"Strength does not come from winning. Your struggles develop your strengths. When you go through hardships and decide not to surrender, that is strength."

"What is the point of being on this Earth if you are going to be like everyone else?"

"Just like in bodybuilding, failure is also a necessary experience for growth in our own lives, for if we're never tested to our limits, how will we know how strong we really are? How will we ever grow?"

"For me, life is continuously being hungry. The meaning of life is not simply to exist, to survive, but to move ahead, to go up, to achieve, to conquer."

"Help others and give something back. I guarantee you will discover that while public service improves the lives and the world around you, its greatest reward is the enrichment and new meaning it will bring your own life."

"If you want to turn a vision into reality, you have to give 100% and never stop believing in your dream."

"The resistance that you fight physically in the gym and the resistance that you fight in life can only build a strong character."

Richard Branson: Born 18 July 1950

Richard Branson gave out his innate desire to become an entrepreneur at a very young age. And, at the age of just 16 years, he made a magazine called *Student*. In the year 1970, he created a mail-order record business. And, after a time, he opened a chain of record stores, called *Virgin Records* which was later called *Virgin Megastores*, in the year of 1972. The entire Virgin brand grew rapidly through the 80s, and he set up the *Virgin Atlantic* airline and also broadened the record label he had already begun.

Branson was knighted at Buckingham Palace for "Services to Entrepreneurship" in 2000. He gained this accolade for his amazing work in the retail, music, and transport industries. In the year of 2004, he founded an actual spaceflight corporation named *Virgin Galactic*. It is well-noted and inspirational for its more-than-intriguing *SpaceShipOne* project.

Richard Branson's Inspirational Quotes:

"*My interest in life comes from setting myself huge, apparently unachievable challenges, and trying to rise above them.*"

"Business opportunities are like buses, there's always another one coming."

"The brands that will thrive in the coming years are the ones that have a purpose beyond profit."

"You don't learn to walk by following rules. You learn by doing and by falling over."

"Entrepreneurial business favors the open mind. It favors people whose optimism drives them to prepare for many possible futures, pretty much purely for the joy of doing so."

"To launch a business means successfully solving problems. Solving problems means listening."

"My definition of success? The more you're actively and practically engaged, the more successful you will be."

Bruce Lee: November 27, 1940 to July 20, 1973

For those who knew him personally, he was said to be a truly magnificent and wonderful man. Lee was known as a true figure of both power and great humility.

Here Are Bruce Lee's Top Tips for Leading a Purposeful & Successful Life:

1. Apply What You Learn

"Knowing is not enough, we must apply. Willing is not enough, we must do."

How many people do you know that read a lot of books and spend a lot of time buying courses, but never apply the knowledge they learn?

You may even notice these tendencies in your life. It's hard to take action and apply what you learn, because we're all afraid of failure, and taking action can be paralyzing, from time to time.

However, real success in life or business doesn't happen until you use the knowledge that you have inside of you. Most of us have exactly what we need to get to our goals, but we make excuses not to even get started.

2. Learn, Discard, Create

"Absorb what is useful, discard what is not, add what is uniquely your own."

It's all well and good to learn from others, but it's not until you take action that you discover what works and what doesn't.

When you discover what doesn't work, you simply discard it and keep going. When you keep moving forward, you can then create your own path.

Living a successful life is all about experimenting and trying new things. The more things you try, the closer you get to true success.

3. Simplicity

"Simplicity is the key to brilliance."

If you can simplify your life, your goals, and your tasks, you will not only be happier, you will also get more done and become more successful.

It was not until I started focusing on one single task and one major goal in my life, that I started seeing rapid results in the direction of my dreams.

If you're trying to go after multiple things at once, you may end up accomplishing none of them. Pick one thing that's the most important to you, and go after that.

The funny thing about focusing on one goal is that it seems that you're neglecting all the other aspects of your life, but when you focus on one goal, magically the other aspects of your life improve, sometimes dramatically.

4. Break Barriers

"Using no way as way, using no limitation as limitation."

It's true, we all have negative beliefs that stop us from being as successful in life as we would like.

The only person holding you back; is you. Once you become comfortable with overcoming your own fears, you will start seeing dramatic success in your life.

One of the most common characteristics of successful people is that they are willing to try new things and face their fears. They are not fearless, but they are willing to do what it takes.

5. Be Open-Minded

"Take no thought of who is right or wrong, or who is better than. Be not for or against."

There's no right or wrong in the universe. It's subjective.

Getting caught up in the drama of who is right or wrong, or who is better than whom, will only distract you from reaching your goals and creating a successful life. There's no need to compare yourself to others, at all.

Stay open to new possibilities, and the viewpoints of others. You can never know what you will learn when you explore things that you (at first thought) believed were pure nonsense.

6. Contribute

"Real living is living for others."

It wasn't until I found my passion, and started contributing to the world with my writing, that I actually started feeling fulfilled.

We all have our unique gifts that we can use to make the world a better place. These are usually talents and skills that you have. These are things that you are very good at, and that you like to do.

It doesn't matter if you like to make jewelry, or if you enjoy cooking, because everything is connected to everything else.

You are here to make a difference with the talents you have. There's a reason why you are you.

7. Manage Your Time

"If you love life, don't waste time, for time is what life is made up of."

We are surrounded by distractions, such as e-mail, Twitter, and Facebook, as examples. They are great at connecting us to each other, but they distract us from what is truly important.

Learn to manage your time, and get the most valuable tasks done before you start to "play."

You can often double, triple, or even quadruple your productivity by using just a few simple, easily learned, time management techniques.

A good one that I use is to write down the three most important tasks for the next day before I go to bed.

8. Be Flexible

"Notice that the stiffest tree is most easily cracked, while the bamboo or willow survives by bending with the wind."

Life will throw curve balls at you, so you have to get used to being flexible. The more comfortable you can be with being uncomfortable, the faster you will grow as a human being, and the more success you will have in life.

This is exactly what distinguishes successful people from unsuccessful ones. Successful people are more willing to be uncomfortable, because they know that it is the fastest path to their goals.

Whenever you bump into something that makes you feel bad, stay flexible, and find the positive lesson or trait in the situation. I've found that most of the problems in my life are actually blessings in disguise.

The only things separating positivity from negativity is time and focus.

9. Set Goals

"A goal is not always meant to be reached, it often serves simply as something to aim at."

If you want to create your dream life, or start a business around your passion, you first have to know what you want. For the longest time, I avoided setting goals, because I thought it was unnecessary.

It wasn't until recently that I discovered that goal setting can not only make me more productive, it can also dramatically increase the clarity I have.

When you set goals, use the S.M.A.R.T criterion, which stands for: Specific, Measurable, Attainable, Realistic, and Timely goals.

10. Be Patient

"A quick temper will make a fool of you soon enough."

One of my weaknesses is my impatience. However, I've learned to channel my impatience into getting more done and becoming more productive.

It's also important to realize that most of the things that are truly valuable in life, take time.

For example, I discovered that creating an online business usually takes anywhere from 3 to 5 years, if your goal is a full-time income.

Whatever you do, keep taking small steps each day toward your primary goal, and you will be surprised at how much you can accomplish in just a few years.

11. Kill the Box

"All fixed set patterns are incapable of adaptability or pliability. The truth is outside of all fixed patterns."

It's easy to get into a rut, which is simply a familiar pattern that feels comfortable. If you truly want to grow as a person and lead a successful life, you have to get out of the 'box.'

In fact, throw the box out altogether, and start following your heart, wherever it leads you. This can be as simple as following your highest excitement in the moment.

Most people are stuck in their minds, and never listen to their heart's deepest desire.

12. Control Your Thoughts

"As you think, so shall you become."

What you think about, you draw into your life. If you're constantly being negative, you will draw more negativity into your life.

Instead of focusing on the negative, think about what you want to get out of life, and focus on the positive aspects, always.

This is another way of telling you that you have to set goals and focus on those goals as often as possible. The results you will get by doing this will be dramatic.

Most people sit around whining about their miserable life, and then they wonder why nothing good ever happens to them.

13. Take Action

"If you spend too much time thinking about a thing, you'll never get it done."

Don't overanalyze and over think. Take massive action even if things aren't perfect, before you start.

Most people that try to get things perfect never get started at all.

I used to be a perfectionist, but I realized that by taking action, I could get much more done and make much more progress.

I also realized that people don't want perfect. They just want solutions to their problems.

14. Allow

"I'm not in this world to live up to your expectations and you're not in this world to live up to mine."

It's easy to get stuck on what other people would think of you if you became successful. Most people are so afraid of this that they never rise above mediocrity.

It is not up to you to make people happy. You can only make yourself happy, and the way others react is just the way they will react.

Don't let other people dictate how you live your life. Determine what you want, go after it, and don't look back. This creates real, lasting happiness.

15. Create Your Own Destiny

"To hell with circumstances; I create opportunities."

You can make all the excuses in the world, but nothing happens until you stop blaming your circumstances, or people in your life, and then you can truly take control of your life.

It is up to you to take responsibility for your life and create your own opportunities. You may not be able to do exactly what you want right now, but you have the opportunity to take steps toward it.

No one will create the dream life for you. You have to do it yourself.

16. Be You

"Always be yourself, express yourself, have faith in yourself, do not go out and look for a successful personality and duplicate it."

As I said earlier, you were born with unique talents, skill sets, and gifts. When you try to be someone you're not, you will only attract people into your life that are not in harmony with you.

When you are you, and that includes the weird things about you, you will find that the most amazing and interesting people start popping up in your life.

Sometimes, this may take years, and sometimes it can happen in just a few days. Let whatever happens be okay, and go with the flow.

17. Have Integrity

"Knowledge will give you power, but character respect."

No success in life is worth it, unless you have integrity.

It's very hard to find people that are honest and have integrity as one of their highest values. It's easy to throw in a lie here and there and try to manipulate people.

Only conscious people realize that this won't make anyone happy in the long term. It might get you what you want in the short-term, but it's not a recipe for happiness.

Live with integrity, and people will respect you. And best of all, you will respect yourself too, which is a very desirable character trait.

18. Learn the Rules, Break the Rules

"Obey the principles without being bound by them."

If you want success in life, learn what other successful people have done to get to where they are.

It's important to learn the principles of success, but not be bound by them. Once you know what you need to do, follow your heart and your intuition.

If you want to learn how to create a profitable website, for example, I recommend you sign up for a training course, and follow the instructions step-by-step.

Once you start seeing success, you can start breaking the rules and begin experimenting.

19. Do Things for You

"Showing off is the fool's idea of glory."

Life is not about impressing other people. If you try to show off, it often backfires.

And if you try to seek the approval of others, it will just make you miserable. The only person that needs to approve of you, is you.

This goes hand in hand with many of the quotes above. You can only be you, and it is not until you reclaim your unique self that you can be truly great.

20. Believe in Yourself

"You just wait. I'm going to be the biggest Chinese Star in the world."

Last, but definitely not least, are the expectations you have of yourself. Your beliefs will determine the success you have in life.

There are ways to overcome limiting beliefs and negative expectations, but nothing happens until you accept that they exist within you.

And nothing happens until you take full responsibility for the life that you have created in this very moment.

Earl Nightingale: March 12, 1921 to March 25, 1989

Earl Nightingale was born on March 12, 1921, and died on March 25, 1989. He was a US radio speaker and author, who spoke about subjects of human character development, including motivational topics, and the purposeful meaningful of existence in the world. His voice was famous in the 1950s on *Sky King*, being the true hero of a radio adventure series, there. He also enjoyed being a WGN radio program host from the years 1950, right up until 1956.

Nightingale was also the renowned author of *The Strangest Secret*, which was rightly termed "...one of the great motivational books of all time." He was a brilliant man who gained much attention from his peers.

The following words are beautiful quotes of wisdom and were taken from Earl Nightingale's essay, aptly called, "Lead the Field."

1. "If the grass is greener on the other side it's probably getting better care."

2. "Each of us creates his or her own life, largely by our attitude."

3. "You can control your attitude. Set it each morning."

4. "It is our attitude toward life that determines life's attitude toward us. We get back what we put out."

5. "Others treat us as we treat them. They react to us. They only give us back a reflection of our own attitude."

6. "Most people begin their day in neutral. They will simply react to whatever confronts them."

7. "Gratitude and expectancy are the best attitude."

8. "...our outlook on life is a kind of paint brush and with it we paint our world. It can be bright and filled with hope and satisfaction or it can be dark and gloomy. The world we experience is a reflection of our attitude."

9. "Don't take the attitude of waiting for people to be nice to you – be nice to them."

10. "Be positive, cheerful, grateful, and expectant."

11. "Always keep that happy attitude. Pretend that you are holding a beautiful fragrant bouquet."

12. "Don't wait for change. You change."

13. "Develop and project an attitude that says 'yes' to life."

14. "You must radiate success before it'll come to you."

15. "Treat every person as the most important person on earth. To them, they are the most important person."

16. "People don't have great attitudes because of great success, they have great success largely because of great attitudes."

17. "Don't catch the bad and infectious attitudes of others."

18. "Before you can achieve the kind of life you want, you must think, act, talk, and conduct yourself in all of your affairs as would the person you wish to become."

19. "Ask yourself every morning, 'how can I increase my service today?'"

20. "Goals reflect your choice of destination."

21. "Most people don't know what they want. Do you?"

22. "Set worthy goals. Don't drift along as a wandering generality. Be a meaningful specific."

23. "Success is not a destination, but a journey. Anyone who is on course toward a worthy goal is successful. Success does not lie in the achievement of a goal but in its pursuit. Success is a journey!"

24. "One thing a goal must do is fill us with positive emotion when we think about it. The more intensely we feel about a goal the more progressively we'll move toward it."

25. "Control your thoughts. Decide about that which you will think and concentrate upon. You are in charge of your life to the degree you take charge of your thoughts."

26. "Spend one hour every day thinking about your goal and how to get there."

27. "Don't waste time thinking about needless things."

28. "Whatever it is you seek in the form of rewards, you must first earn in the form of service. Each of us serves a portion of humanity, all those with whom you come in contact."

29. "Every-time we use a product or service, someone is serving us."

30. "Think not about future rewards but about present service."

31. "Find what you can do best that renders service to others and do it with all your might."

32. "Make the best use of what you have and what you are in the time you've been granted."

33. "We are at our very best, and we are happiest, when we are fully engaged in work we enjoy on the journey toward the goal we've established for ourselves."

34. "Put in motion the right cause, and the right effect will take care of itself."

35. "Life can only return to you that which you sow. What do you have to sow? You have great wealth; you can think, you have talent, and you have time."

36. "Money is the harvest of our production and service. We, in turn, use it to obtain the production and service of others."

37. "Money is an effect. It is the result of a cause, and the cause is valuable service."

38. "We will receive not what we idly wish for, but what we justly earn. Our rewards will always be in exact proportion to our service."

39. "Success is the progressive realization of a worthy ideal."

40. "Failures… believe that their lives are shaped by circumstances… by things that happen to them… by exterior forces."

41. "Think of a ship with the complete voyage mapped out and planned. The captain and crew know exactly where the ship is going and how long it will take - it has a definite goal. And 9,999 times out of 10,000, it will get there."

42. "The human mind is much like a farmer's land. The land gives the farmer a choice. He may plant in that land whatever he chooses. The land doesn't care what is planted. It's up to the farmer to make the decision. The mind, like the land, will return what you plant, but it doesn't care what you plant."

43. "Everything that's really worthwhile in life came to us free — our minds, our souls, our bodies, our hopes, our dreams, our ambitions, our intelligence, our love of family and children, and friends, and country. All these priceless possessions are free."

44. "Success is not the result of making money; earning money is the result of success — and success is in direct proportion to our service."

45. "Your world is a living expression of how you are using and have used your mind."

6

YOU REAP WHAT YOU SOW

IT WOULD BE SUCH A INJUSTICE TO REWORD THIS FAMOUS speech by Earl Nightingale so in this chapter i will include this man speech word for word. This is by far the most amazing eye opening information i have ever read and it changed my view on life and changed it immensely. There is a youtube video of it if you're more audio attuned - The Strangest Secret by Earl Nightingale

A few years ago, the late Dr. Albert Schweitzer (Nobel Prize winner) was asked in an interview, *"Doctor, what's wrong with men today?"* The great doctor thought for a moment, and then he replied, *"Men simply don't think!"*

This is what I want to talk about with you. We now live in a golden age and an era which humanity has strived to reach, and even dreamed of, and looked toward for a few thousand years. We now live in the wealthiest period which has never existed on the face of the earth... it has become "a land of a full chance and unprecedented prosperity," for everybody.

Nevertheless, if you take 100 people, starting at the age of 25, do you understand what will happen to them by the time they reach the age of 65? These 100 individuals believe they will become successful. They are enthusiastic in life, and there is a sparkle in their eyes. Actually, they walk proudly, and growth appears to be a motivating adventure for them.

But, once they actually reach 65, only 1 of the 100 will have become wealthy, and only 4 will have become financially independent; 5 will have to carry on working; 54 will be financially unstable and dependent on others for their life's needs.

It is a fact, that only 5 out of 100 will succeed and make the grade! What is the reason so many fail? What became of the sparkle when they were still 25? What happened to their dreams, their hopes, and all their plans? And why is there such a massive inconsistency amid what these people wanted to do, and what they actually accomplished?

True Definitions of Success

First, we must explain success, and here is the most fitting definition I could find: *"Success is the progressive realization of a worthy ideal."*

- Success can be a school teacher who is now teaching, since that's what he (or she) wanted to do.

- Success is an entrepreneur who started his own business; that was his/her dream and what he/she chose to do.
- Success is a salesperson who desires to be the top salesperson in their chosen company, and make motions on pursuing that goal.

To be a success, quite literally, denotes anyone who has realized a worthy predestined ideal, and then got to do what they chose to do... intentionally. Nonetheless, only 1 out of 20 achieves that! The remaining are "failures."

Distinguished psychiatrist Rollo May wrote a delightful book titled "Man's Search for Himself," and in his book, he says, *"The opposite of courage in our society is not cowardice... it is conformity."* And here lies the reasoning for numerous failures. Conformity and people falling in line with everyone else, without even understanding why, or where they are headed.

We have learned to read by the age of 7 years. We can learn to make a living by the time we're 30, or younger. In most cases, by that time, we're not only making a living, but we can also support a family.

However, by the time we're 65 years old, we still haven't learned how we can become financially independent in a land that is the richest we have ever known. Why is this? We conform! The vast majority are acting like the wrong proportional group, and are included in the ones who never succeed, to their success "wants" and "ideals."

Goals

Have you ever wondered why a lot of people work hard and without honestly accomplishing anything in particular, and why other individuals seem to work less, and always seem to get everything? They appear to have the "magic touch." You've probably even heard the saying, *"Everything he touches turns to gold."*

Have you observed a person who turns out to be successful? Have they ever negated the need to become more successful? And, on the flip side, have you noted how someone who tends to fail continues to fail?

The difference is their goals. People who have goals most often prosper well, because they know where they are heading. It's a simple fact. Failures tend to believe their lives are designed by circumstances and by situations that happen to them, instead of because of them.

Think of a vessel that has a whole voyage planned and mapped out. The captain knows precisely where the ship is heading and what it takes to reach their specific goal. And, in the majority of cases, it will get there.

Now, if you take another vessel and not put a crew in it, or a captain to direct... well, it might not go far. It will probably float around endlessly. If we give it no destination, and just start the engines and set it on its way, then there is no place for it to be directed to.

I think you'll agree that; if it manages to leave the harbor, there's a good chance it will sink or find itself on a deserted beach. It is unable to go anywhere, really, because it has no destination and no guidance. It's the same thing with humans, it's a pretty simple concept, but very important to master.

Today's society can be portrayed as a convoy in wartime. The whole society slows down as a way to protect its weakest link. Similarly, a naval convoy needs to go at the slowest speed that permits the slowest vessel to maintain formation.

It is for these reasons that it's easy to make a living in today's society. No particular skills, forethought, or talents are required to support a family. We have a level of what we call "security." So, if we wish to succeed, all we have to do is decide the level of security we want, and how high above it we want to aim.

All through history, wise men, philosophers, prophets, and teachers have had disagreements with each other on various things. It is only on this definition that they think alike, and are in broad and unanimous agreement.

The Secrets to Success and to Failure Are:

We Become What We Think

This isn't actually a secret. It was first broadcast by the earliest wise men, and it makes an appearance throughout the Bible on numerous occasions. Very few people have come to learn it or understand this fact.

This is why it seems strange, and why for some compelling reason it (practically) remains a secret.

The great Roman Emperor Marcus Aurelius said, *"A man's life is what his thoughts make of it."*

Disraeli quoted, *"Everything comes if a man will only wait... a human being with a settled purpose must accomplish it, and nothing can resist a will that will stake even existence for its fulfillment."*

William James stated, *"We need only in cold blood act as if the thing in question were real, and it will become infallibly real by growing into such a connection with our life that it will become real. It will become so knit with habit and emotion that our interests in it will be those which characterize belief."* He continues, *" ... only you must, then, really wish these things, and wish them exclusively, and not wish at the same time a hundred other incompatible things just as strongly."*

Dr. Norman Vincent Peale versed it another way. He said, *"If you think in negative terms, you will get negative results. If you think in positive terms, you will achieve positive results."*

George Bernard Shaw broadcast it as, *"People are always blaming their circumstances for what they are. I don't believe in circumstances. The people who get on in this world are the people who get up and look for the circumstances they want, and if they can't find them, make them."*

Well, it's pretty evident, don't you think? We will become what we think. A person who believes in a solid and worthwhile goal will take every endeavor to reach it, because that's what he's thinking about. Non-stop thinking, if it involves a passion.

On the other hand, a person who has no goals, and no idea where they're going, will have thoughts of confusion, worry, anxiety, and fear. From these thoughts, they will thereby create a life which replicates these thoughts. If a person thinks of nothing... they themselves become nothing.

Sowing the Seed

The human mind can be likened to a farmer's land. The land presents the farmer with choices. He can plant whatever he chooses. The land has no care what is planted.

It is the farmer who makes his decision. The human mind, like the land, returns whatever is planted, and there is no concern about what you sow. And, if the farmer plants a few seeds and as many poisonous plants, what can happen to the land or the crops which try to survive?

Don't forget, the land *doesn't* care. It will grow poisonous plants just as bountiful as it will corn. So, as it says in the Bible, and regardless of your religious beliefs, "As ye sow, so shall ye reap." In simple terms, don't plant poison in your mind.

The human mind is far more productive and mysterious than earth. Nonetheless, it works similarly. There is no care of what we plant, be it success or failure. And many great teachers and spiritualists have taught this. So, do we choose to think about a concrete and worthwhile goal, or confusion, fearful circumstances and beliefs, and/or anxiety-driven perspectives? But then... whatever we plant will return to us.

Our mind comes as standard equipment when we are born. It comes with no charge, and thoughts which are given freely. But, we tend to place very-little value on these. It is the things that cost us, and we pay money for, these are what we value. This fact is unfortunate, but true, for most individuals.

A simple paradox is, everything in life which is worthwhile comes to us free: our minds, souls, hopes, dreams, and our ambitions are all valuable possessions... and are free.

Materialistic things which cost money are fundamentally cheap and are replaceable at any time. A man can be entirely wiped out and go on to create another fortune, in time. He can do this many times over. Even a home, if it falls down, can be rebuilt. It is the things we received for nothing which we can never replace. Good health is also one.

The mind can do whatever job is assigned to it. Generally speaking, we use it for smaller jobs rather than big ones. Now is the time to decide. What do you want? Plant a new goal in your mind.

It will be the most important decision you can ever make.

Do you feel the need to excel at your current job? Do you wish to go places inside your company, or in your local community? Do you want to become wealthy, or healthier?

All you need to do is plant the seeds in your mind, tend to it, and work progressively forward and toward your goal, and they will, in time, become a reality.

Sir Isaac Newton said, with regard to the laws of gravity, *"If you jump off the top of a building, you always go down, and never go up."*

Other laws of nature are the same. They continually work. Contemplate your goal in a relaxed and confident way. Imagine yourself in your mind's eye as already achieving your goal. Picture yourself performing the things you will perform once you've reached your goal.

Each of us becomes the sum of our own thoughts. We are where we think we are, because that is where we choose or feel we deserve to be. This happens even if we admit it or not. We must all live off the fruits of our thoughts, and what you think in the near-future molds your life and determines your long-term future. You are, in reality, guided by your mind.

Our thoughts must be controlled, and it is the same rule which leads people toward lives of success, wealth, and all the things they dream of. Likewise, the very same law can drive a person into the gutter.

Since the dawn of recorded history, experts have told us to: pay the price, and become the person you wish to become. In truth, it's nowhere near as hard as living unsuccessfully.

As soon as you decide on a specific goal to work toward, you immediately develop into a successful person with a growth mindset. Now you're in that rare collection of people who see where they're going, long-term. Out of every 100 individuals, you can now belong in the top 5.

Don't worry too much about the details of *how* you're going to achieve your goals. Actually, in truth, once you make the shift in perspective then that will come from a power higher than yourself. Sometimes, even in daydreams and passionate thinking. Remember, passion is the key.

The most crucial aspect is to know where you're going. Answers will flow to you of their own accord, and when the time is right.

There is no excuse to not start today. There is nothing to lose, and you have everything to gain… and your whole life ahead of you to win. I know you can do it.

7

30-DAY PLAN

Over the next 30-days, I want you to follow all these steps until you have reached your goal.

Step 1:

Write on a card what you wish for, more than anything else. It might be more money, or maybe you'd like to double your income. It could be a larger and more beautiful home. It might be job success, or it might be a particular stance in life. It could be even something as simple as a more balanced family life.

Write down the specifics of what you want. Make sure you have a single, defined goal. Carry this with you, so you are able to look at it several times during the day.

Think of it in a happy, relaxed, and confident way every morning when you get out of bed. Now you have something to work toward, and also a reason for getting out of bed... and because it's something you're passionate about, you really *do* have something to live for.

Every available chance you have during the day, look at your card as well as just before retiring for the night. When you look at it, remember your obligation to become what you think about.

Step 2:

You must stop thinking about your fears. Every time fearful or negative thoughts enter your mind, replace them with positive thoughts and how they relate to your worthwhile goal.

There might come a time when you feel like quitting, sometimes it is easier for humans to think negatively, rather than positively. This is the reason only five percent go on to be successful! Start now and place yourself in this group.

Dorothea Brande said, *"Act as though it were impossible to fail."*

Step 3:

Your personal success is always measured by qualities and quantities of services you render. A vast number of people will tell you, they wish to make more money, without fully understanding this law.

Success isn't the end result of making money, when we talk about wealth creation. Earning money are the results of success, and our success comes with a direct proportion to our services.

A considerable number of people look at this law backward. It's like a man who stands by a stove and says, *"Give me the fire, and then I'll add the wood to it."*

How many individuals do you know, or are there today, who take the same approach toward life in general? There are many millions.

Fuel has to be provided, before we can expect any return of heat. Equally, we need to be of service, before we can expect to receive any money.

Don't be concerned with the money. Be of useful service and build, work and create! When you do this, you will come to find there's no limit to prosperity and abundance which will come to you, eventually.

If you find that you fail during your first 30 days (suddenly finding yourself consumed by negative thoughts), just start again from the point you reached and give yourself 30 more days.

Progressively, your new habits will begin to form until you find you are one of that ideal minority. One who finds that virtually nothing is beyond their reach.

But, more than anything else; please don't worry! With worry comes fear, which is crippling. The one major thing which causes worry throughout your test is attempting to do it all yourself. And also doing something you are not passionate about.

All you need to do is hold your goal in front of you, and everything else will slowly take care of itself. Partake in this 30-day secret, and then repeat it... and repeat it again.

Each time it'll become ingrained in you, until you start to wonder how you ever lived any other way. Live with this new mentality, and floodgates of opportunity will open for you, leading you to more riches than you might have dreamed existed.

Money? Yes, there will be plenty of it. More importantly, you will have peace... and you will be a part of the minority who can lead a calm, happy, and prosperous life. If I could remind you of 3 things, I would reiterate for you to stay positive, set small goals, and follow your passion, always.

IN CONCLUSION

Thank you so much for joining me here in this title. It's great to look at some interesting research, and at the heroes in history (and of our current time), to get our mindset right. Once we realize that the shift needs to occur, we can actually begin to implement those changes as is necessary. And in time, we will begin to see our wealth accumulating, over time. It's true; mindset is everything. And, it's also true that having a winning mindset that's similar to other rich people is crucial. Additionally, and essentially, that is the one thing that all millionaires and billionaires have in common.

We need to set goals for ourselves. In fact, it's these intrinsic goals which catapult us to work harder and to persevere with more success. Goals drive your daily motivation, and this aids in helping you to diligently thrive to meet them. This factor is important. Goals intrinsically drive a person to succeed. You might be learning how to drive, or getting a degree, starting a new business, writing a book, or even collaborating in a partnership. Remember, taking small steps in increments to achieve goals really helps us to keep up with the positive, growth mindset attitude that is needed. Additionally, becoming overwhelmed by attaining a huge goal quickly isn't advised, and taking small, steady steps to get the smaller ones done is crucial. The desire to accomplish a goal is what keeps people going, even on the "bad" days.

So, in closing, I am wishing you every success in your future, all you need to do is think rich, and never doubt yourself, no matter what the circumstances are. I hope you can use this resource to gain motivation, because that's why I wrote this title, after all. And so you can live out your dreams of wealth creation and so much more!

You are only ever limited by your imagination...

I am sending my warmest thoughts this very day, warm regards, *James.*

"*Stay in line with your passion, it will set your whole world on fire.*" - James Moore.

Made in United States
Orlando, FL
16 June 2022